ROI

MW01122731

Who Were the Ancient Romans?

The beginnings of Rome are uncertain. But nearly 3,000 years ago shepherds were settling on hillsides near the Tiber River in what is now central Italy. In time, settlements spread to other nearby hills and then into the valleys between the hills. The settlements merged into the small city-state of Rome in about 753 B.C. The people were a mix of Etruscans from the north and Latins from the south. Together they became known as Romans. From about 550 B.C. Rome was ruled by Etruscan kings. But in 509 B.C. the Romans drove the king out, and Rome became a tiny independent republic. A republic is a government in which the people, not a king or queen, have ruling power. Rome, like Greece, spread its influence over distant lands and was the center of a huge empire.

HIGH STANDARD OF LIVING

Both riches and slaves were brought to Rome from other places in the empire. A few Romans were truly rich and lived in luxury. Most had a simpler but comfortable life.

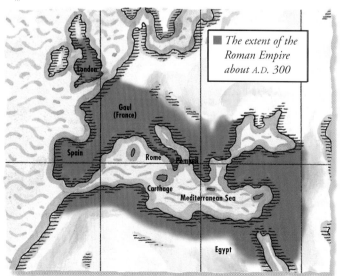

The extent of the Roman Empire about A.D. 300

London

Gaul (France)

Spain

Rome

Pompeii

Carthage

Mediterranean Sea

Egypt

A NIGHT ON THE TOWN

The Romans learned much from Greek architecture. But they were able to build higher, more magnificent structures by perfecting a strong arch. Many of their buildings are still standing today. Most Roman towns had huge amphitheaters for public entertainment. Here people could see plays, sporting events, and gladiator fights.

THE MIGHT OF ROME

Rome had an almost unbeatable military. No other civilization had ever developed such well-organized forces. The most respected were the foot soldiers, who had to be Roman citizens. They were grouped into legions of about five thousand men. Non-Romans living within the empire were led by Roman officers. After their service they were awarded citizenship.

ROMULUS & REMUS

Legends say that Rome was founded by the twin brothers Romulus and Remus. They were sons of the Roman god Mars and the daughter of King Numitor. A wicked uncle ordered the twins drowned at birth in the Tiber River. But kindhearted servants put them in a basket and floated them downstream. When they washed ashore, a she-wolf (above) heard their cries. She fed them with her own milk to keep them alive. Then a shepherd found them and raised them as his own. Later they were reunited with their grandfather, King Numitor. As adults, they fought over who should rule Rome. Romulus killed Remus in 753 B.C. to become king.

LATIN LANGUAGE

Most people in ancient Rome could not read or write. But the rich and powerful read and wrote formal Latin. Many educated Romans also knew Greek. As the culture and influence of Rome spread to other lands, Latin spread as well. It is the basis of many modern languages.

HEARTH & HOME

The house of a wealthy Roman was built around the atrium. This was a large open-aired room with columns and often a fountain or pool in the center. Each house also had a shrine to the gods (right). Early Romans believed some gods dwelled within their homes. For example, Vesta, the goddess of the hearth, was thought to live in the fireplace.

READING & WRITING

The wealthy could afford to hire tutors to teach their children to read and write. This girl is using a wax tablet. To write, she would scratch the letters into the wax with a stylus made of metal or bone.

HOME COMFORTS

Many of the richest Romans had two houses. One was in town, where matters of business and state were handled. The other was in the country, a welcome escape. Homes were designed to keep cool. They had few windows to let in the heat. Floors and walls were kept cool with stone or marble tiles. These often had stunning mosaic inlays (left).

TAKING IT EASY

The Roman ideal called for a few elegant furnishings in beautifully decorated rooms. This couch would have been used for an afternoon nap. It would also have been used at mealtimes. Romans reclined rather than sat while eating.

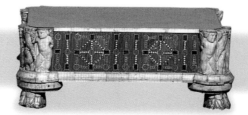

Life for the Rich

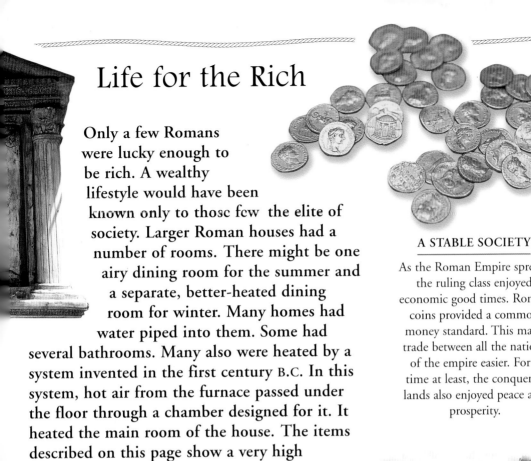

Only a few Romans were lucky enough to be rich. A wealthy lifestyle would have been known only to those few the elite of society. Larger Roman houses had a number of rooms. There might be one airy dining room for the summer and a separate, better-heated dining room for winter. Many homes had water piped into them. Some had several bathrooms. Many also were heated by a system invented in the first century B.C. In this system, hot air from the furnace passed under the floor through a chamber designed for it. It heated the main room of the house. The items described on this page show a very high quality. Thousands of years would pass before civilizations once again enjoyed such a high standard of living.

A STABLE SOCIETY

As the Roman Empire spread, the ruling class enjoyed economic good times. Roman coins provided a common money standard. This made trade between all the nations of the empire easier. For a time at least, the conquered lands also enjoyed peace and prosperity.

SOCIAL STANDING

The easy life of the rich was only possible because of the hard work of slaves. Prisoners from conquered lands were forced to work the fields or become servants in wealthy households. Society had three layers: citizens; noncitizens, who had fewer rights; and slaves, who had no rights at all.

THE FORUM

The central meeting place in a typical Roman town was called the forum. It began as a simple open marketplace. The forum grew into an important center of business and social activity. At its busiest, the Roman forum was very crowded and very noisy.

Life for the Poor

CREATURE COMFORTS

The poor had few comforts or luxuries. Housing was usually in bad repair and had no plumbing. People lit their small rooms with oil lamps like the one above. Town dwellers often had to use public toilets. Few could afford to use the public baths, since they were not free. Water from public fountains, however, was both clean and free.

The Roman world had startling contrasts. A few wealthy and powerful Romans lived in splendor. However, most people had to work hard for little gain. If they lived in the country, they squeezed from the land what they could. If they lived in the city, they worked for low wages and often found themselves in debt. They lived in apartment buildings stacked four or five stories high. Many of these were owned by wealthy landlords who did not keep them in good repair. There were frequent fires in these dirty buildings. Sometimes overcrowding would cause the buildings to topple. One Roman leader expressed a common attitude of the powerful toward the poor. He thought of the great masses of people as "a troublesome neighbor." Some leaders supplied the hungry masses with corn to keep them from revolting.

LIFE IN THE TOWNS

In the towns most poor people lived in cramped, low-quality buildings called *insularae,* or islands. They were surrounded by streets, as islands are surrounded by water. The apartments were built over open-fronted shops. Townspeople earned their livings by providing a service or trade, working in shops, or serving as government clerks. This picture shows what is left of a typical town street in Pompeii, in southwest Italy. It was noisy and busy in its day.

LIFE IN THE COUNTRY

Most country dwellers were poor. They scratched out a living on small family farms. They kept cows for their milk (to drink and to make into cheese). They kept poultry for eggs. All members of the family were expected to work, including the children. The men looked after the livestock and carried out heavy tasks, such as plowing. Women tended the crops, looked after the house and family, and made clothes. The children helped with chores wherever they could around the farm.

FARMING CHANGES

As the Roman Empire spread, farmers in conquered areas had to change the way they farmed. They could no longer just grow enough food to feed themselves. Instead, they needed to grow enough extra to pay tributes and taxes to the Roman government. Also, patterns of land ownership changed. Often the rich and powerful acquired farmlands and had slaves do all the work, sometimes in chains. Farming became a business.

FAMILY LIFE

Family life was very important to the Romans, whether rich or poor. There were no government programs to take care of the elderly poor, so few could afford to stop working. When they did stop, their care fell to family members.

Food & Drink

Compared to other ancient peoples, Romans from all classes ate and drank well. The poor, however, had less food and less variety of food than the rich. The poor in the country lived mainly on grains and vegetables. They grew cabbages, parsnips, lettuce, asparagus, onions, garlic, and radishes. They ground grain and used the flour to make round loaves of bread. Sometimes they flavored the bread by baking olives, onions, garlic, or cheese into it. The poor in the city usually did not have ovens in their apartments because of the risk of fire. They often picked up ready-made bean stews or vegetable and meat pies from nearby shops. The rich, however, often ate grand meals. Eggs, cheese, or shellfish might come first. Then came the main course, often featuring fish. Exotic foods such as flamingos stuffed with dates were also popular. Fruits and pastries finished off the meal. Romans used no forks, so finger bowls were kept on the table to keep hands clean.

THE SPICE OF LIFE

Roman food was often very spicy. Parsley, thyme, fennel, fenugreek, angelica, and mint were some of the common spices. Another favorite flavoring was the sweet and sour mix of fruit, honey, and vinegar. Spices were often used to hide the taste of spoiling food. Keeping food fresh was hard to do.

RECLINING DINING

Rich Romans, like many ancient peoples, reclined for meals. Dinner guests shared couches that had room enough for everyone to recline.

EVERYDAY DRINKS

Romans of all classes relied on wine as their main drink. The wealthy drank better quality wine. The poor settled for a type of wine similar to vinegar. Wine of any type, however, was always drunk with water. It was considered improper to drink undiluted wine. It was also considered uncivilized to drink milk. Milk was thought to be good only for making cheese.

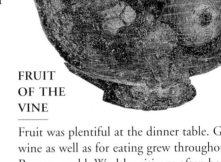

OLIVES

One of the principal crops grown in the Roman world was olives. They are still grown on many of the lower slopes in Mediterranean regions today. Olives had many uses. They were eaten whole, as appetizers, or crushed for their oil. The oil was squeezed out by pressing the fruits (left), in much the same way grapes were pressed for wine. The oil was used for cooking and salad dressings. It was also used for burning in lamps and for massaging into the skin as a beauty aid.

FRUIT OF THE VINE

Fruit was plentiful at the dinner table. Grapes for wine as well as for eating grew throughout the Roman world. Wealthy citizens often had their own private vineyards. Roman wine came in four main varieties: black, red, yellow, and white, both dry and sweet. Romans frequently mixed wine with other ingredients, such as herbs or honey. The sour grapes were often used to make a mild vinegar used for salad dressings and sauces. Spoons like the gold and silver ones shown here were probably used to serve wine mixed with water. These spoon handles are shaped like dolphins. Spoon-shaped strainers were also used to filter wine. Spoons were probably also used to eat eggs and shellfish. Their pointed handles were perfect for getting snails from their shells.

HOME COOKING

A volcano destroyed Pompeii in A.D. 79. Lava and ashes buried and helped preserve many everyday items. This impressive stone oven from Pompeii shows how food was cooked in the kitchen. The fire underneath the stove was fueled by wood or charcoal. The round openings on the top were probably covered by grills to allow several pans to be used at once.

DRAMA

Most towns had an amphitheater where dramas were performed during a festival. Only men could become actors, and most of the actors were slaves. Women's roles were played by boys. The players wore masks to represent their characters. In later eras, women were able to take part in popular but crude pantomimes.

BLOOD SPORTS

Romans loved to watch blood sports. Game days might begin with fights of animals against people, or animals against animals. (Five thousand wild animals were slaughtered in just one day when the Colosseum first opened.) For the midday entertainment, there were public executions. The evening's sport were the gladiator fights. Condemned criminals or slaves had to fight one another, usually to the death.

CHARIOT RACING

Nothing thrilled the Romans like chariot racing. Chariot racers were professionals and belonged to rival factions. The factions were named for the colors of the drivers' outfits: the blues, greens, reds, and whites. Violence often broke out between fans of one faction and fans of another after a race.

THE COLOSSEUM

The Colosseum in Rome was the greatest amphitheater ever built. It could seat 50,000 people. Its brilliant design depended on the use of arches. This design gave it so much strength that it could stand on its own. (Most others were built into a hillside for support.) The Colosseum had a specially built floor that could be filled with water so sea battles could be acted out.

Pastimes

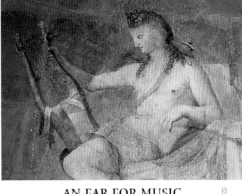

Entertainment was a prized part of Roman life. The Romans had many gods to worship, so there was almost always a feast day to celebrate. The festivals often included theater, dramatic sporting events, and musical performances. Attendance at these wildly popular events was always free. The festivals were paid for with a mix of public and private money. Rulers saw the events as a way to keep the masses happy and earn their loyalty. The wealthy also enjoyed going to the public baths. These were like today's health clubs. People could exercise, visit with friends, and relax in the heated waters.

AN EAR FOR MUSIC

All religious ceremonies included a flute player. The purpose of the music was to drown out any impure words or sounds, so the gods could not hear them. This picture shows Apollo, the god of light, poetry, and music, playing the stringed lyre.

GLADIATORS

The most spectacular event at the Colosseum was the gladiator fights. Gladiators were usually criminals or slaves who were specially trained to fight. Some fights included many gladiators. Some women also were trained to be gladiators.

Fashion

The Roman Empire spanned nearly 700 years. During that long period of time, fashions gradually changed. But the importance of keeping cool in the hot climate never changed. Everyday clothes were loose fitting and made from light materials. The rich could buy silks from China or cotton from India. But most people wore clothes made of homespun flax or wool. Middle-class women did the spinning and weaving for their families. The rich used slaves. Poor city-dwellers had no time to spin their own cloth or make their own clothes. So they often bought their clothes in shops. Children did not have their own fashions, as they do now. As in most societies, clothes reflected attitudes. Women, for example, had to be covered from head to foot when they went outdoors. Among state officials, purple stripes of different widths showed degrees of rank. Only the emperor could wear a totally purple toga.

FOOT LOOSE

People wore sandals indoors. The open design helped keep feet cool. For the outdoors, people needed covered shoes made of tough leather. The roads were dusty and dirty. Some styles of footwear had leather thongs that laced around the calves.

MIRROR, MIRROR

The Romans made mirrors by polishing pieces of metal to a high shine. Most were made from silver or bronze. The back of this mirror was finely decorated.

CHANGING FACE OF FASHION

Rich Roman women looked to the emperor's wife for their hairstyles. Whatever she wore, they wore. It was also stylish to look pale. Some women applied chalk dust as a face powder. Others wore wigs of real hair. Blond hair from captured slaves was especially popular.

LOOKING GOOD

Women of all classes wore jewelry. The rich wore gold and silver necklaces, bracelets, armlets, anklets, and earrings. These were often decorated with jewels or rare stones. Hairpins were another way to add dazzle. People with less money had to make do with bronze jewelry adorned with colorful glass beads. Both men and women wore rings.

THE TOGA

The toga was the national dress of Rome. It was usually made from a very large piece of white wool. Its size made it heavy and hot to wear. Its color made it hard to keep clean. So the toga was usually worn only for formal occasions among the rich. Togas were worn often enough, though, to keep the local cleaners busy. They were called fullers. They used human urine to bleach the clothing.

FOLLOWERS OF FASHION

The earliest Romans copied Greek ideals of fashion, including long hair and curly beards. As time went on, however, the clean-shaven look became popular. Barber shops sprang up throughout the cities. For everyday clothes, both men and women wore loose-fitting tunics. Tunics were usually cut from one large piece of material. Women wore long robes called stola over their knee-length tunics. They fastened these with a shoulder brooch or fancy pin. For men, trousers were considered uncivilized.

Art & Architecture

WALL PAINTINGS

Fine wall murals decorated the country homes of the rich and the many temples of Rome. They were usually painted directly onto the plaster, so few have survived. They portrayed dramatic stories from Roman mythology. But they often displayed a vivid realism.

Roman architecture grew out of Greek building styles. The Romans, however, added their own details and improvements. For example, Roman buildings have the same basic column styles as the Greeks'. But between the columns the Romans added rounded arches. Rows of connected arches were the key to the Romans' massive buildings. Romans were also among the first to use cement. They found that a reddish volcanic soil added great strength to the cement mixture. The addition also made the cement very quick to dry. Roman builders could construct sturdy walls at a much quicker rate than before. The Romans built on a grand scale. On the inside of buildings, they created a stately beauty. Marble sculptures of the gods and famous citizens were displayed in public buildings. Walls and floors were decorated with mosaics and paintings. Romans also created life-like portraits.

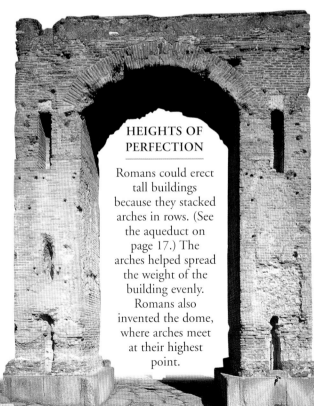

HEIGHTS OF PERFECTION

Romans could erect tall buildings because they stacked arches in rows. (See the aqueduct on page 17.) The arches helped spread the weight of the building evenly. Romans also invented the dome, where arches meet at their highest point.

MOSAICS

Many Roman buildings were decorated with mosaics on the floor or walls. Mosaics are pictures made from small square stones set carefully into wet plaster to form an image. Some were black and white. Others used bright-colored, shiny stones. Skilled mosaic layers called on the wealthy with pattern books from which to choose a design. Mosaics were made to last, and many have survived.

FORTIFICATIONS

Huge walls surrounded most Roman towns and cities. When the empire reached Britain, the emperor Hadrian built a huge defensive wall right across the country from east to west. It was built along a route where many forts already stood. The wall was 73 miles (117 km) long, 15 feet (4.6 m) high, and 10 feet (3 m) thick. Watchtowers were built along the wall so intruders could be spotted.

TOOLS OF THE TRADE

The plans of Roman architects called for precise measurements. These pictures show a few of the tools for precision. On the left is a bronze square for measuring angles. The dividers (right) were used to transfer measurements from the plan onto stone.

EPHESUS

Wherever the Romans conquered, they tore down old buildings and put up new ones in the Roman style. They also built or repaired roads leading to the conquered cities. These ruins are from Ephesus in western Turkey. Many of the civic buildings at Ephesus have survived. Shown here is the library of Celsius.

Health & Medicine

To the Romans, good health came with cleanliness, honor to the gods, and, when necessary, help from doctors. Romans practiced personal cleanliness at the baths. Their clean water supply and drainage systems also limited the spread of disease. Romans honored the gods by praying, visiting shrines, and wearing charms to ward off disease. Still, they turned to doctors for help with many everyday complaints. Until Caesar's time, doctors were not held in the high esteem they are today. Most were foreigners, especially Greek, so they were not even citizens. Others were slaves or former slaves. They used herbal remedies for common illnesses. But they were helpless against serious disease, and many Romans died in epidemics. Doctors performed surgery, but they used no painkillers. Most army legions had their own doctors who traveled with them to tend the wounded. As the armies conquered new lands, the medical knowledge of the doctors spread.

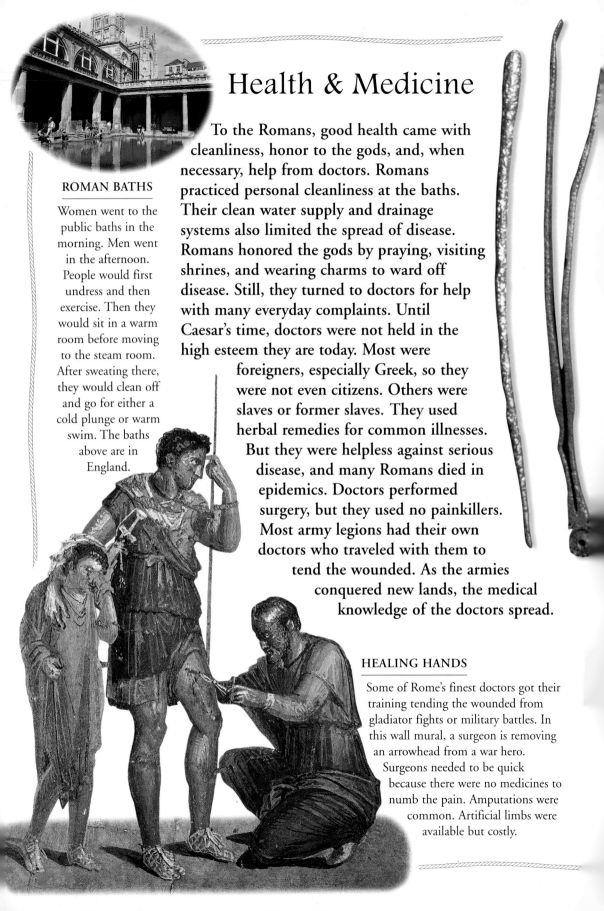

ROMAN BATHS

Women went to the public baths in the morning. Men went in the afternoon. People would first undress and then exercise. Then they would sit in a warm room before moving to the steam room. After sweating there, they would clean off and go for either a cold plunge or warm swim. The baths above are in England.

HEALING HANDS

Some of Rome's finest doctors got their training tending the wounded from gladiator fights or military battles. In this wall mural, a surgeon is removing an arrowhead from a war hero. Surgeons needed to be quick because there were no medicines to numb the pain. Amputations were common. Artificial limbs were available but costly.

THE APPLIANCE OF SCIENCE

These instruments were used for surgery. They include knives, scalpels, and hooks as well as spatulas for mixing and applying balms. Early on, doctors were permitted to operate on criminals to learn about the human body. Later that practice was outlawed, and they used animals instead. Still, the human body was little understood. Many patients died from shock, trauma, or infection after an operation.

FRESH WATER

Romans built this aqueduct at Nimes in France to get water across a valley. Water flowed through a channel at the top. Then 13 lead pipes carried the water to different parts of the town.

PERSONAL HYGIENE

This hair comb was made of ivory. It probably belonged to a rich person and may have been used to remove head lice. The poor were also careful to keep themselves groomed. Shaving was painful because blades were dull. Some men plucked out their beards instead.

NATURE'S CURE-ALL

Cabbage was a favorite ingredient in herbal remedies, which often worked very well. Another was garlic. Soldiers were given a daily dose to improve their well-being. Romans also used "magical" chants. The phrase *huat huat huat ista pista sista dannabo dannaustra,* repeated over and over, was believed to help mend dislocated joints.

CLEAN WATER SUPPLIES

The Romans had an advanced water supply system. Clean water from reservoirs in the countryside flowed into the towns. There was no way to stop this flow. So the Romans also developed a drainage system to take waste and extra water away.

GOD OF FERTILITY

Bacchus, the Roman god of wine, was also the god of fertility. He is often associated with merrymaking and wedding feasts. As the figures in this carving show, parties sometimes became unruly when people drank too much wine.

CUPID'S ARROW

Cupid was the son of Venus, the goddess of love and beauty. He carried a magical bow and arrow. If Cupid shot arrows into the hearts of a man and a woman, they were said to fall hopelessly in love.

THE WEDDING CEREMONY

Wedding ceremonies were often led by women priests. After an animal sacrifice, the couple would join right hands and give their consent to the marriage. Marriages were arranged by families. But if the couple felt a strong dislike for one another, they could be excused. Deep love often grew between husband and wife after they were married awhile.

THE GODDESS DIANA

Diana was a Roman goddess. She is often pictured with her bow and arrow because she was goddess of the hunt. Sculptures and paintings show her as a strong, athletic woman. Diana was also the goddess who protected unmarried girls. Even after marriage, women valued her powers. People often made sacrifices to her before a woman was to give birth. They hoped that these offerings would ensure a safe delivery and healthy child.

GIRL POWER

This detail is from a wall carving at Pompeii, in the "Villa of Mysteries." It shows the ceremony of a young woman as she enters into a life of religious service. Men who became priests were allowed to marry. But women priests had to be chaste and unmarried.

Love & Marriage

To the Romans, marriage was a sacred relationship, the foundation of a family. Only children born into a legal marriage could become citizens. On her wedding day, the young bride, often no more than 13 years old, put aside the toys of her youth. She put on a white toga with a reddish veil. At the ceremony, which took place at the bride's house, the couple sat on the skin of an animal that had been sacrificed to the household god. The sacrifice was to make sure the bride would be welcomed into the groom's house. Then the couple shared a wedding cake and served it to friends. After the ceremony, a parade of boys and flute players took the couple to the groom's house. The bride rubbed oil on the doorposts and then tied a wool cloth to each. The groom picked her up and carried her in. Marriage had begun.

DUTIFUL WIVES

Women were expected to be dutiful wives. But they held positions of great respect within the household, sharing duties with their husbands. Unlike Greek wives, they lived in the same room as their husbands and ate dinner with them. But they could not take part in public life.

DEVOTED COUPLE

The Greek colony of Etruria in northern Italy was an early influence on Roman civilization. This magnificent Etruscan casket cover dates back to the sixth century B.C. It comes from the tomb of a devoted husband and wife who share the same grave.

Women & Children

Although many mothers and wives were much respected, women did not enjoy the same rights as men. Under the law, they were treated as children. They were unable to own property or hold legal control over their children. They had to obey a male guardian their whole lives. Fathers, husbands, uncles, or other males made decisions for them and their children. Most girls could look forward to little more than a life of hard work. In the home, women did spinning and weaving, cooking, laundering, and cleaning. In the fields, they carried out the lowly jobs. Only wealthy children received an education. Many girls put aside their lessons at age 12 and were expected to learn how to keep a household running smoothly. Boys were often educated beyond that and groomed for a good job. Some women found jobs in the city, working as hairdressers, bakers, clerks, or waitresses. The lucky few, and only the rich, might become respected priestesses.

CHILDBIRTH

Some women made a living as midwives. Giving birth was dangerous, and many babies and mothers died. Until about A.D. 300, fathers had the legal right to abandon a baby, letting it die outside. But usually the birth of a child, especially a boy, was a joyous event. Offerings of thanks were made to the gods.

WORKING ON THE LAND

Most country dwellers had to work hard just to meet their basic needs. The menial jobs were performed by women and children. These included sowing seeds, tending the crops, feeding the poultry, collecting the eggs, milking the cows, and making cheese. As the large farms of the wealthy spread throughout the empire, some poor farmers lost their lands and had to go to work for others.

PLAYTHINGS

Children had a variety of toys often made of wood or bone. These pieces are from a game like dominoes. Boys liked to play with lead soldiers. Girls enjoyed rag dolls.

THE VESTAL VIRGINS

Girls from wealthy families were chosen to tend the shrine in Rome to the goddess Vesta. They also guarded other sacred objects believed to protect Rome. They had to serve for 30 years. The state paid their expenses, but required them to remain virgins.

JUNO

The patron goddess of women was Juno. She is often shown seated, as in this fine statue. There is usually a peacock, her symbol, beside her. Juno is a very motherly figure. She was thought to protect women, especially during childbirth. Originally, she was the goddess of the moon, the queen of heaven.

SONG & DANCE

Romans adopted the Egyptian goddess Isis. She was thought to have powers over the cycle of life. This carving shows women and children dancing in tribute to Isis. They would also read from sacred books and shake rattles in her honor.

CHILDHOOD

This child wears a *bulla* (lucky charm) around his neck. It would have been given to him at his naming ceremony nine days after his birth. Its purpose was to keep away evil and help the boy grow up with a good character. A boy would wear this charm until his wedding day.

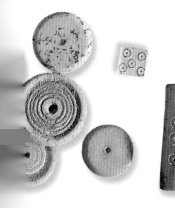

War & Weaponry

AUGUSTUS
(63 B.C.–A.D. 14)

Caesar's adopted son was known as Augustus. He ruled brilliantly after Caesar was murdered. In 31–30 B.C. he defeated Antony, one of his own generals, who with Queen Cleopatra, was trying to win control over Egypt.

For a while, the Romans copied the fighting style of the Greeks. They fought with long spears in closed ranks for protection. Male property owners between the ages of 17 and 46 were called into service as needed. When the battle was over, they went home. But around 260 B.C., a series of bitter wars began. These lasted more than 100 years. More soldiers, and better-trained fighters, were needed. So the Roman government created a paid army. Citizens who joined had to stay in the army for 16–25 years. They became very experienced fighting with various weapons, especially daggers and swords. By A.D. 50 Rome ruled all nearby lands. Rome stayed in control by keeping an army in each conquered area.

GALLEYS

Roman warships, known as galleys, had huge battering rams on their bows meant for ramming enemy ships. They played a key role in the war between Augustus and Antony. Augustus was the first to create a permanent navy.

HANNIBAL

In their drive to invade North Africa, Romans faced a brilliant general named Hannibal. He marched his army with 40 elephants through North Africa, Spain, and across the Alps to Italy. He led a surprise attack against Rome itself. He was defeated in 202 B.C.

PRIDE OF ROME

A Roman legion consisted of about five thousand infantrymen. These legions were the pride of the empire's army. Only citizens could serve in them. In command of each legion was a centurion. He wore a distinctive helmet, like this one. It was complete with crests or plumes so he could be easily seen and followed in battle. Noncitizens fought in groups that protected the flanks of a legion and scouted ahead. They also served as foot soldiers at frontier forts. There they protected the empire from attack or rebellion.

MIGHTY EAGLE

Each legion had a soldier who had the high honor of carrying a statue of an eagle into battle. The eagle was a symbol of Roman might. The eagle bearer sometimes used the eagle to motivate tired and frightened soldiers. When the Romans attacked Britain in 55 B.C., they were reluctant to leave their boats. The eagle bearer jumped into the water and began wading toward shore. He held the eagle up and told his troops to follow for the glory of Rome. They did.

JULIUS CAESAR

Civil war broke out as generals competed for power. Julius Caesar (about 100–44 B.C.) declared himself supreme ruler. He made many improvements in Rome. But he was murdered by his fellow senators who believed he had become too powerful.

ROMAN WEAPONS

Most soldiers carried an iron or steel dagger and sword, a short bow, a javelin, and a throwing spear. One of their best weapons, though, was the excellent training they got. They practiced with weapons that were heavier than the real ones. In that way, the real ones seemed easier to handle.

SIEGE ENGINES

The most common Roman siege weapon was the *ballista,* shown here. This mighty weapon could hurl a large boulder more than 100 feet. It was also used to throw bundles of burning sticks and straw onto enemy ships.

Crime & Punishment

Beginning in 509 B.C., Rome was a republic. Senators and other public officials were elected. Only the wealthy, however, got the top government positions. At the Senate, officials debated issues and made decisions as representatives of the citizens of Rome. Each city had an elected council of about 100 men, who usually held office for life. Citizens who were not elected officials also met in assemblies and discussed the issues of the day. After 27 B.C., Rome was ruled by emperors. The Romans had courts where crimes and grievances were heard. Punishment very often took the form of payments or exile rather than prison time. Criminals, even Roman citizens, were sometimes sentenced to slavery. Roman law sought fairness, at least by ancient standards. Law was defined as "the study of the good and just."

THE NEW REPUBLIC

Augustus declared Rome a "new" republic and himself its first emperor. He learned from Julius Caesar's mistakes. Augustus tried not to appear too grand. He began many building projects that put the people of Rome to work. He won the respect of the people.

CRUCIFIXION

Crucifixion was a horrible punishment. It was saved for those who posed a serious threat to the empire. Death was slow and painful. Usually the victim's arms were tied above his head onto a single pole. Sometimes they were fastened to a cross with their arms outstretched. Either way, the lungs gradually collapsed, cutting off air supply.

CORRUPTION

The Romans took pride in their constitution. They believed it was the most democratic of any nation in the known world. However, the system was open to abuse. Leaders often pushed through laws to win the loyalty of the people and stay in power. Rival generals tried to gain control through their friends in the Senate. As the power of Rome began to fade, many senators fell victim to bribery by rich merchants.

TRIAL BY COMBAT

Many criminals were forced to battle in the Colosseum (above). If they survived, they might win their freedom. Romans were amused by watching them fight for their lives in the arena against animals or gladiators. The word *arena* comes from a Roman word for sand. The Colosseum had a thick layer of sand to absorb all the blood that was shed.

THE PRICE OF HOMAGE

This coin shows Augustus receiving a child from a conquered person. Emperors expected to be honored with offspring. Those who refused to give up their children in homage were killed. Many conquered people became slaves. Julius Caesar once sold 50,000 newly captured slaves in one lot to a slave trader.

DEATH BY EXECUTION

Many crimes carried severe punishments. This picture shows some of them: death by sword, axe, and stoning. Once an official was killed by a slave. That slave and 400 other slaves in the household were killed as punishment.

ALL ROADS LED TO ROME

Roman roads were made of stone blocks or cobbles above a gravel bed. There were drainage ditches on both sides. When possible, Romans built long, straight roads to reduce traveling time. The army built many of the roads on its march to conquer distant lands.

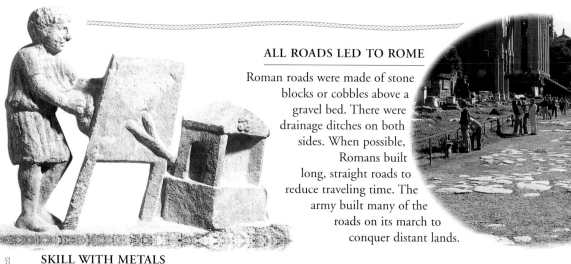

SKILL WITH METALS

The Romans were skilled metalworkers. They made metal tools, weapons, utensils, jewelry, and coins. They knew how to mix copper and tin to make bronze. They added zinc to the bronze to make a metal that looked like gold.

SEA POWER

Roman seafaring did not begin until the growth of the empire. At that time the Roman navy became the major power in the Mediterranean. There were no compasses. So sailors found their bearings with landmarks during the day and the stars at night. They avoided sailing at all in the stormy spring and winter months.

LIGHTHOUSES

The ruin of this Roman lighthouse is on the cliffs of Dover in England. Fires at the top were the source of light. Mirrors of polished bronze reflected the fire. The reflection made the light bright enough to guide ships.

ROAD TRANSPORT

Merchants took their goods to market on pack animals or in carts pulled by oxen or horses. Chariots were used for warfare and later adapted for the famous and dangerous races.

Transport & Science

The Romans were inspired by the Greeks. But they also went further to develop many of their own advances, especially in technology. They recognized the importance of a clean water supply to good health. So they perfected a system of piping and drainage in their towns and villas. With this system in place, Romans were able to add other advances. The public baths with their steam rooms and hot pools were one innovation. Another was the hypocaust, a clever under-floor heating system. In building matters, they invented a new form of very strong concrete and improved the way bricks were made. They figured out how to make stone arches by first building a wooden frame in the size and shape they wanted. Then they added stones cut to the precise shape and connected them with strong mortar. When the whole structure was completed, they would remove the wooden frame. The arch would then stand on its own. Roman arches were the strength of Roman bridges, aqueducts, and other public works. But perhaps the greatest success of the Roman Empire was its impressive network of roads. The roads once used to move soldiers and supplies to distant parts of the empire are still used today.

WARM BATHS

Pictured above is the hypocaust under the Roman baths at Carthage, built between A.D. 145 and 162. The floor was raised on the pillars shown here. Hot air from adjoining furnaces passed through the spaces. Grills in the floor above let the hot air rise and heat the rooms.

CENTRAL HEATING

The hypocaust heated both the water and the rooms of private houses and public baths. This view shows how the system worked. The fires are where the furnaces were. Hot air from the fire rose and flowed through the chambers under the floor.

Religion

Many of the gods in the Roman world were borrowed from ancient Greece. The Romans gave them different names, all except Apollo, god of the sun. Also, the Romans had a different attitude toward their gods. The Greek gods had familiar human qualities, but the Roman gods were distant and fearsome. Temples and shrines, supported by the government, were everywhere. Romans had no sacred writings, so they had no creed to accept. As long as they performed rituals correctly, they were honoring their gods. Romans were also open to the gods and religious beliefs of the peoples they conquered. Romans sent to guard the outlying regions of the empire often adopted the local customs and beliefs. In the late A.D. 200s, Christianity was thought to be a threat to Rome. Gradually, though, some Romans became Christians. By about A.D. 337 Christianity had become the main religion of the Roman Empire.

GODDESS OF WISDOM

Minerva was the Roman goddess of handicrafts and wisdom. She is often shown in a warlike stance, as is the Greek goddess Athena. Minerva stood for the power of the empire. She was a favorite figure to decorate the shields and armor of men fighting for Rome.

MITHRAISM

Mithras was the Persian god of light. Followers, only men, believed he was sent to earth to slay a godly bull. From the bull's blood came all creatures of the earth. Many soldiers in the Roman army adopted Mithraism.

GOD OF WAR

Mars was the Roman god of war. He is usually shown as a powerful soldier clad in full armor. The month of March is named in honor of him. He was the second most powerful god, after Jupiter. After taking power, Augustus Caesar had a huge temple built in Rome to honor Mars for Rome's military victories.

KINGS OF THE GODS

The most powerful of all the Roman gods was Jupiter. He was thought to have lived on the Capitol Hill in Rome itself. He was the god of light and the sky. His symbols were thunder and the eagle.

FEMALE CULTS

A few Roman religions were just for and about women and fertility, such as Cybele, Isis, and Vesta. This picture shows the temple of Vesta, in Rome.

CATACOMBS

Early Roman Christians may have used catacombs as a secret meeting place. The original purpose of these underground tunnels was as burial places. The bodies were put in chambers cut in the walls. The rock-cut tunnel in this view leads to the shrine of a Roman prophet, the Sybil.

CHRISTIANITY

The Romans executed Jesus Christ in about A.D. 33. Soon after, his followers, called Christians, began spreading the news that Jesus had risen from the dead.

SACRIFICES

Sacrifices to the gods marked many Roman life changes. Marriage, the birth of a child, an illness—all were times for animal sacrifices. The sacrificial altar is shown at left.

Legacy of the Past

Ruins of huge stone civic buildings, temples, and villas tell only part of the story of Roman life. As a whole, Roman society was rich and brilliant in technology. Only a very few enjoyed a lifestyle suggested by the majestic ruins. However, the Roman Empire did leave a legacy that has lasted up to the present day. Many European roads, for example, are built over old Roman roads. Modern plumbing and sewage systems owe much to Roman engineers. Roman architecture and city planning have been copied throughout the Western world. Such modern languages as Spanish, French, Italian, and Portuguese came directly from the Romans' Latin. Many other languages, including English, have strong Latin influences and use the Latin alphabet. Roman law and the idea that a large area could be united under one rule helped shape nations and empires to the present day.

ROAD BUILDING

Perhaps the greatest Roman legacy was in engineering, especially in road making. Many of today's roads follow their original Roman course. They needed little improvement until the 1800s.

CLASSIC DESIGNS

Few complete Roman buildings survive anywhere. But their remains have inspired builders through the ages. The government buildings in many of today's capitals show the influence of classical Roman designs. The Capitol building in the United States, for one, borrows Roman style.

THE EMPIRE DIVIDES

In A.D. 395, the Roman Empire was divided into two parts, east and west. By 476, the Western Empire had fallen to waves of invaders from the north. It had also become fully Christian. The Eastern Empire remained intact for another one thousand years. This Eastern mausoleum shows its Roman heritage in the use of arches and domes.

THE FALL OF THE EMPIRE

In A.D. 406, Germanic tribes invaded Roman territory on the Rhine River border in the north. In 410, Rome itself was sacked. The army was called back from the farthest outposts to defend Rome. But the invasion succeeded. By 476 the Western Empire had fallen.

ATTILA THE HUN (about A.D. 406–53)

The Roman Empire was at its height around A.D. 200. After that it declined. Civil war at home weakened the empire. So did constant attacks along its many borders. One fierce enemy was Attila the Hun, leader of tribes from central Asia. He was so ruthless he became known as the "scourge of God." He extended his territory from the Rhine River to China. In A.D. 447 he defeated the Roman emperor Theodosius.

THE STATES OF MODERN EUROPE

The breakup of the Roman Empire led to the forming of modern Europe. In the north, the Frank invaders settled in what is now France. The Saxons invaded England. In the east, Turkey kept elements of both East and West, as it still does. This picture shows the St. Sophia Mosque in Istanbul.

BURIED IN ASH

Pompeii is a remarkably preserved slice of Roman life. In A.D. 79 the city, located near present-day Naples, was destroyed when the volcano Vesuvius suddenly erupted. For 1,700 years the city and its people lay buried beneath the ash. Modern digs have revealed a city untouched by time. Rich and poor alike were caught in their everyday activities.

DID YOU KNOW?

That the Romans used asbestos shrouds? The Romans knew of the fireproof properties of asbestos. They wrapped corpses in asbestos shrouds before cremating them. In this way, although the body burned within the funeral fire, the ashes were kept separate from the rest of the fire. The body ashes were placed in urns. The vestal virgins are also believed to have used asbestos lamp wicks to ensure that the flame at the shrine of Vesta never burned out.

That pantomime may have its origins in ancient Rome? Every year, just after Christmas, pantomimes are conducted in theaters throughout Europe, where chaos and mayhem are the order of the day. Pantomimes may have their origins in the Roman festival of Kalends, where the everyday world was temporarily turned upside down. Revelers dressed in animal masks and engaged in off-key singing during mock religious gatherings. Men and women changed roles, and humorous verses were recited. The festival was known as the Feast of Fools.

That Rome introduced passports? To ensure the safe passage of merchants and government officials within the empire and through foreign lands, the Romans issued a "certificate of safe conduct," which was shown to the ruler of each country passed through on a journey. The certificate contained words of warning to any foreign official who did not allow the safe passage of its bearer.

That Romans cut the largest stone blocks in the world? At Baalbek, Lebanon, stand the ruins of a group of Roman temples surrounded by a massive stone wall. The three largest stones are known as the trilithon. The stones were cut from a quarry about a mile away and transported and lifted into position about 25 feet (8 m) high. The biggest stone measures 67 feet (21 m) long by about 13 feet (4 m) square and weighs an incredible 800 tons. The stones were laid so precisely that the joints are almost an exact fit. How, and why, the stones were put in position remains a mystery.

That the excavated remains of Pompeii are like a window into the past? When Mount Vesuvius erupted in A.D. 79 the molten lava and hot ash spread so quickly that more than 2,000 of the city's population of 20,000 were unable to escape. The bodies of people fleeing the choking fumes have been discovered in the streets, encased in solidified lava. Some people were killed in midaction, such as a customer being served with a drink in a wine bar and a baker who had just put some loaves into an oven. The remains at Pompeii are still in the process of careful excavation to reveal the everyday lives of ordinary people, frozen in time.

ACKNOWLEDGMENTS

Map of the World: David Hobbs Picture Research: Image Select

Published by Jamestown Publishers, a division of NTC/Contemporary Publishing Group, Inc.

4255 West Touhy Avenue Lincolnwood (Chicago), Illinois 60712-1975, U.S.A.

This edition © 2001 by NTC/Contemporary Publishing Group, Inc. ISBN: 0-8092-9500-8

First published in Great Britain in 1998 by ticktock Publishing Ltd., The Offices in the Square, Hadlow, Tonbridge, Kent, TN110DD.

© 1998 ticktock Publishing Ltd. All rights reserved.

No part of this publication may be reproduced, stored in a retrieval system, or transmitted in any form or by any means without the prior written permission of the publisher. Printed in Hong Kong.

Picture Credits:

t=top, b=bottom, c=center, l=left, r=right, IFC=inside front cover, OFC=outside front cover

AKG; London 10/11, 17br, 23ct, 24bl. Alinari - Giraudon, Paris; 7tl, 9cb, 14bl, 19tr, 31br & OFC. Ancient Art and Architecture; 18cl, 23cb, 22/23ct. Archives Larousse - Giraudon; 10/11cb. Bridgeman Art Library; 16/17ct, 17cr, 18cr, 27br. et Archive; 24br. C.M. Dixon; 9br, 15tl. Chris Fairclough Colour Library / Image Select; 6cr, 15r, 16tl, 30/31c. Werner Forman Archive; 5cr, 4tr, 4b, 4tl, 11tr, 13tr, 18tl, 18bl, 20tl, 20br, 21b, 25c, 27tr, 29cb. Giraudon; 2/3cb, 2tl, 4c, 6b & OFC, 6tl & OFC, 8bl, 8cr, 10r, 12/13cb, 12tl, 14tl, OFCbl, 16bl, 19b, 21tr, 21tl, 25b, 25t & IFC, 26tl, 26bl, 26/27c & OFC, 28c, 28b, 29tr, 30b. Image Select International; 2/3ct, 3br, 3tr & OFC, 5tr, 5cb, 9tl, 10tr, 10tl, 13br, 12/13ct, 12bl, 15br & OFC, 14/15b, 22tl, 29tl, 29c, 30/31c. Erich Lessing / Art Resource; 9tr. Gilles Merme - Giraudon; 18/19ct, 22bl. Pix; 30tl. Ann Ronan at Image Select; 7cr, 7cb, 17tr, 17bl, 22cb, 23r, 23b, 24tl, 26br, 26/27c, 26tr, 28l, 31tr. San Lorenzo Maggiore-capella Di Sant' Aquilino, Milano, Italy / Mauro Magliani / SuperStock; 29br. Spectrum Colour Library; 8tl. The Telegraph Colour Library; 30l. Villa Giulia, Rome, Italy / Canali PhotoBank, Milan / SuperStock; 20bl.

Every effort has been made to trace the copyright holders and we apologize in advance for any unintentional omissions. We would be pleased to insert the appropriate acknowledgment in any subsequent edition of this publication.